Changing Families

A Guide for Kids and Grown-ups

David Fassler, M.D.
Michele Lash, M.Ed., A.T.R.
Sally Blakeslee Ives, Ph.D.

Waterfront Books
98 Brookes Avenue
Burlington, Vermont 05401

Copyright 1988 by Waterfront Books

Third printing, November 1990.

ISBN: 0-914525-08-5 (paperback)
ISBN: 0-914525-09-3 (plastic comb)

Distributed to the book trade:
THE TALMAN COMPANY
150 Fifth Avenue
New York, NY 10011
1-800-537-8894

Library of Congress Cataloging-in-Publication Data

Fassler, David.
    Changing families.

    Summary: Provides advice on coping with such family changes as separation, divorce, remarriage, new family members, and new schools.
    1. Stepparents—Juvenile literature. 2. Remarriage—Juvenile literature. 3. Brothers and sisters—Juvenile literature. [1. Divorce. 2. Remarriage. 3. Step-parents] I. Lash, Michele. II. Ives, Sally Blakeslee 1945-   . III. Title.
HQ759.92.F37 1987   646.78   87-40470
ISBN 0-914525-08-5 (pbk.)
ISBN 0-914525-09-3 (soft)

Contents

On Using This Book

This book is about families and some of the changes they can go through. Separation, divorce, and remarriage are a few of the difficult transitions families may experience. We know that such events can be confusing for both children and adults. We wrote this book to help families talk together about the thoughts and feelings associated with these changes.

Changing Families can be used by children from ages 4 to 12. A child may choose to read the book alone, or with the assistance of a parent, teacher, counselor, therapist, or other caring adult. When sharing this book with a child, it is important to be accepting, flexible, and sensitive to his or her responses. The book does not attempt to address all situations or provide all answers. Instead, it is designed to introduce issues and enhance the expression of concerns and questions. Children should be allowed to explore the book in their own way, covering material in any order and at their own pace. Used in a supportive context, *Changing Families* can facilitate open and honest discussion about difficult topics.

Suggestions for Parents

1. Explain to the child that this is a different kind of book, one in which he or she can share feelings and thoughts through both drawings and words. Unlike school books or library books, this is a book in which to write and draw.

2. Young children may need to have the book read aloud. For some, it may be best to read the book in several sittings.

3. Let the child know that he or she can have a safe place in which to store the book. Make sure the child has access to the book.

4. Let the child work on the book at his or her own pace, and choose the order in which to complete the chapters. Children will use the book in many different ways.

5. Make sure the child has access to writing and drawing materials.

6. If you are reading the book with a child, pick a quiet time and a private place. This is a time to concentrate on the child and his or her feelings.

7. Be accepting and nonjudgmental. Let the child know that there are no right or wrong answers or feelings. Accept the child's emotions as valid and important.

8. Some children may wish to read the book without writing or drawing. They may decide to add their own thoughts, comments, and artwork at a later time.

9. When working through the "New Families" section, use it as an opportunity to help the child understand the terms pertaining to his or her own family situation. This can be an opportunity to correct misunderstandings.

10. When the child wants to stop working on the book, respect his or her wishes. You can always return to it at a later point.

11. Parents, stepparents, and other adults may also find the book useful to help them understand the child's perspective in a changing family situation.

Suggestions for School Guidance Counselors and Therapists

Individual Therapy:

1. *Changing Families* may be used in the context of individual therapy to enhance the child's expression of his or her thoughts and feelings. Reading the book can also be supportive and reassuring as the child realizes that his or her experiences are similar to those of other children.

2. Work through the chapters, paying particular attention to the sections most pertinent to the child's situation and emotional status.

3. *Changing Families* is a therapeutic tool, which can be used in conjunction with other expressive techniques such as play, art, music, drama, and movement.

Group Therapy:

1. *Changing Families* can be used as the framework for short-term therapeutic groups.

2. Group sessions can be organized around particular chapters or themes in the book.

3. In the group setting, opportunities can be provided for children to complete the drawing and writing activities suggested in the book.

4. Drawings, stories, poems, and other creative expressions generated by the group of children can be collated and copied for group members.

Suggestions for Classroom Teachers

1. *Changing Families* can help children develop a broader perspective on the variety of possible family situations.

2. When a class contains a number of children from changing families, sharing the book with the entire group can help children begin to talk about their individual situations with their peers.

3. It is best not to identify aloud the children in the class from stepfamilies or divorce situations. Let the identification come spontaneously from the children themselves.

4. Children should not be graded or judged on the activities contained in the book.

5. This book may elicit strong emotions from some children. Use of the book may help identify children who should be referred to the school guidance counselor.

6. *Changing Families* can also be used individually, either by a teacher with the permission of the child's parent, or by recommending the book to a parent for use at home.

Suggestions for Librarians

1. *Changing Families* may be particularly useful for children who do not like to read, or those with a short attention span. The hands-on, interactive format serves to personalize the experience and engage the child.

2. The librarian can help children explore the different ways they might use the book—on their own, with a parent, or with another adult friend or professional.

3. As a workbook, *Changing Families* may present a dilemma for librarians, since children are not traditionally permitted to write or draw in library books. In the library setting, the book can be used as a reference or with adult supervision.

Acknowledgments

Special thanks to:

Marion D. Bauer, Adv. Cert.
Anna Cotton
Nancy Cotton, Ph.D.
Adele D'Ari, M.Ed.
Elise Egerter, M.D.
Ann Epstein, M.D.
Alex Erickson, R.N.
Barbara Kester, Ph.D.
Michael Lash
Judy Logan
Sam Loughridge, C.A.S.
Kathi Newburger, A.T.R.

Paul Organ, M.D.
Mimi Pantuhova, A.T.R.
Rosanne Phillips, M.S.W.
Bob Pierattini, M.D.
Bill Rae, Ph.D.
Amy Rofman
Julie Rofman
Sam Rofman, M.D.
Elizabeth Schmit
Irm Wessel, A.C.S.W.
Morris Wessel, M.D.
Sue Wolf, M.D.

and Alex, Allison, Betsey, Carrie, Heather, Jenny, Katie, Kristopher, Lisa, Mirah, Nat, Sara, and the many other children who shared their thoughts, feelings and creative expressions.

CHAPTER 1

Families

What makes a family a family?

3

A group of people with connections.

People in families help each other.

Families celebrate things together.

7

I Love BirthDays

Happy Birthday!

8

A house is just something that sits there,

but a family is a group of people who love each other.

11

There are many different kinds of families.

Me and my mom.

13

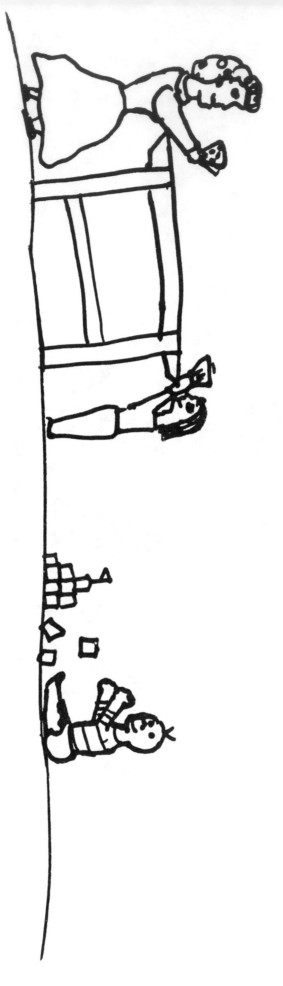

I live with my mom and little brother. We're a whole family.

Draw a picture of your family.

15

Some kids are part of more than one family.

16

My two families.

Me

Me

Sometimes it is even hard to know who is in your family.

18

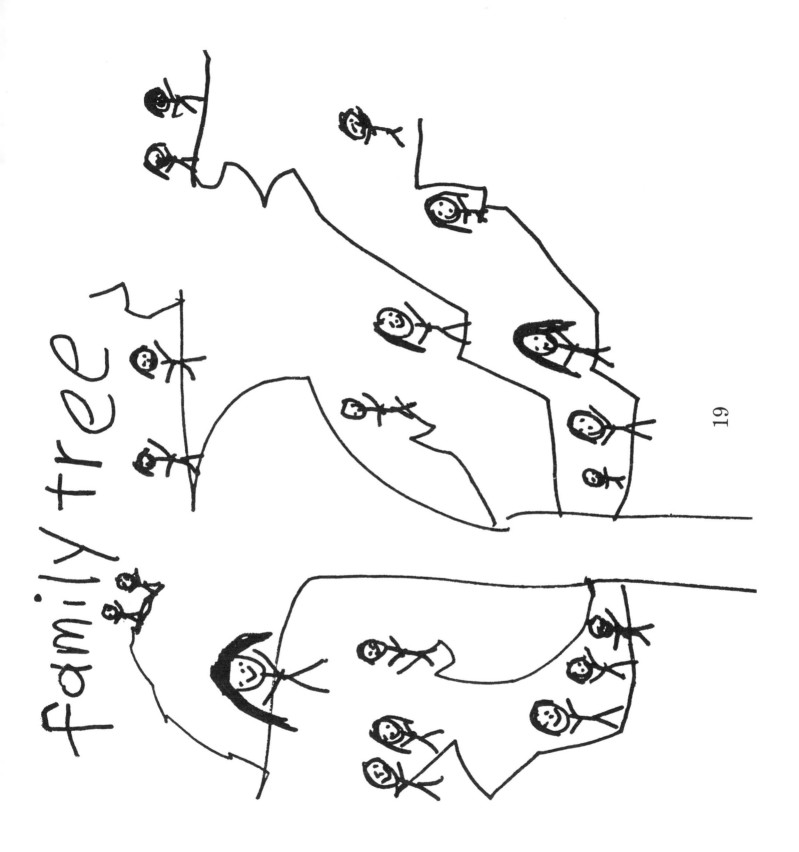

19

CHAPTER 2

Separation

Families can go through many different changes.

What changes have taken place in your family?

We got a new dog.

We moved to a new house.

My mom had a new baby. Now I have a sister.

My grandfather died.

My father lost his job!

I got my big sister's room when she left for college.

Sometimes the changes are not fun at all. Some changes can be pretty scary.

They aren't talking to each other.

Sometimes parents get into fights. Children can feel caught in the middle.

I'm Tired of being caught in The middle.

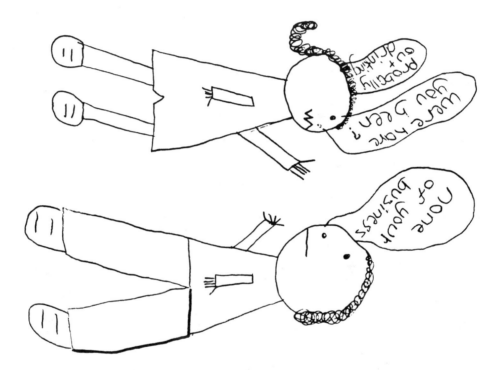

When your parents fight it
feels like it is all your fault,
but it isn't.

My MoM
Kicked DaD
out of the
house.

30

when my parents fight my tummy hurts to hurt.

when my parents fight, my tummy starts to hurt.

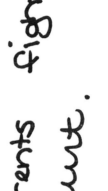

I'm going my room.

Sometimes I have scary dreams.

me

If parents can't work out their problems, they may decide to live apart from each other and figure out what to do about their marriage.

This is called a separation.

33

I was sad when my dad moved out.

When parents separate, kids may have more than one home.
The homes may be very different from each other.

My mom's house is quiet.

My mom's house is loud. My dad's house is quiet.

There are more rules at my mom's house.

My dad has a VCR. We watch lots of movies at his house.

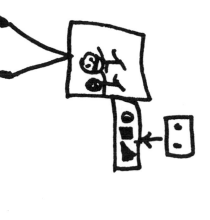

37

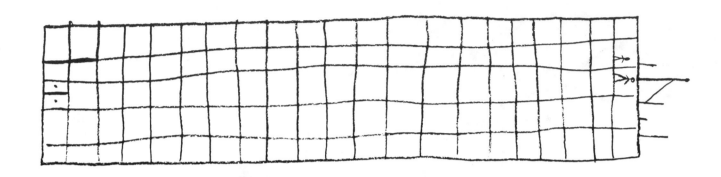

My mom lives in a big
apartment building.

Families may move to new neighborhoods, and kids may have to go to new schools.

moving truck

Are you going to a new school?

Draw your new school here.

41

It's hard to move away from old friends.

It's not the same to talk on the phone.

Sometimes it's hard to make new friends.

Draw a picture of a friend.

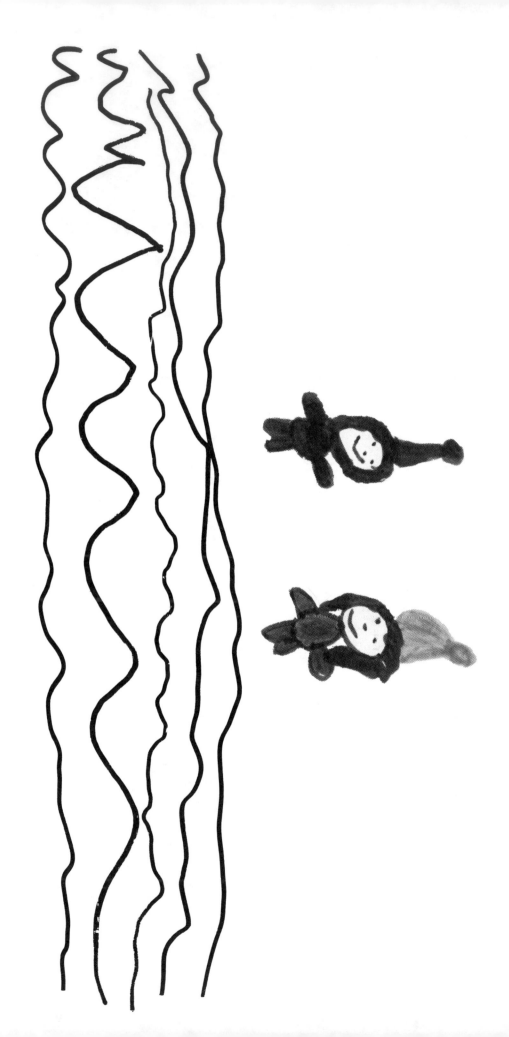

Visiting arrangements can be pretty confusing.

My mom lives far away. I only get to see her at vacation time.

I like staying with my dad and his girlfriend in their new apartment.

I haven't seen my dad for a long time.

I only see my dad Tuesday and Thursday and every other weekend.

It's hard to know when I can play with my friends, because my parents keep changing the visits.

46

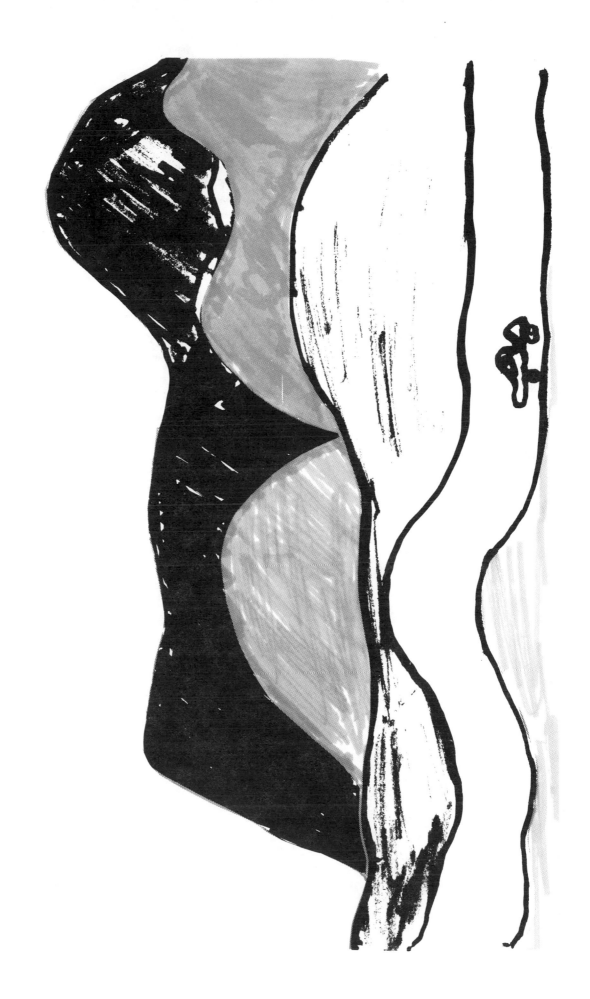

I take a taxi to my mom's house.

48

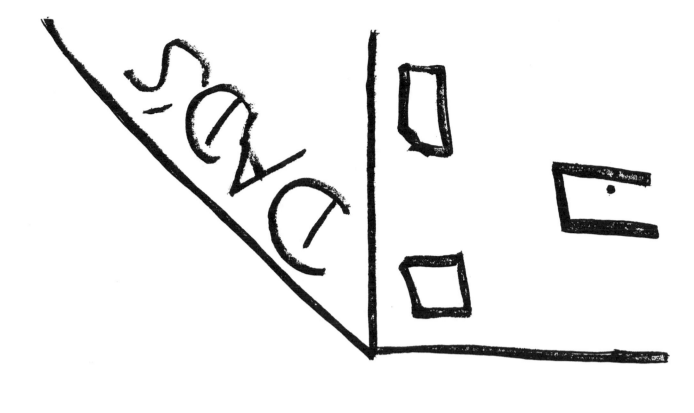

Kids have lots of questions about separation.

Why do people get separated?

I still don't understand why I can't live with my father.

Why did they get married in the first place?

Sometimes, kids don't like the changes in their families.

I don't like our new house.

It's hard to sleep at my mom's place.

Now that my mother has a job,
I have to stay with a babysitter
after school.

I don't get to see my dad enough.

I'm tired of hearing about the money problems.

I MISS MY MOM.

51

After mom moved out, my dad started going out on dates. YUCK!

52

I DON'T LIKE IT WHEN MY MOM'S
BOYFRIEND TELLS ME WHAT TO DO!
HE'S NOT MY REAL DAD, AND I DON'T
SEE WHY I HAVE TO LISTEN
TO HIM.

MOM

MOM'S
BOYFRIEND

ME

Kids also say that some changes feel good.

It feels special to do things alone
with my mom.

Even though I miss my dad, I feel better because at least they aren't fighting all the time.

55

Draw a picture of something you like to do with your dad.

I like to go roller skating with my dad.

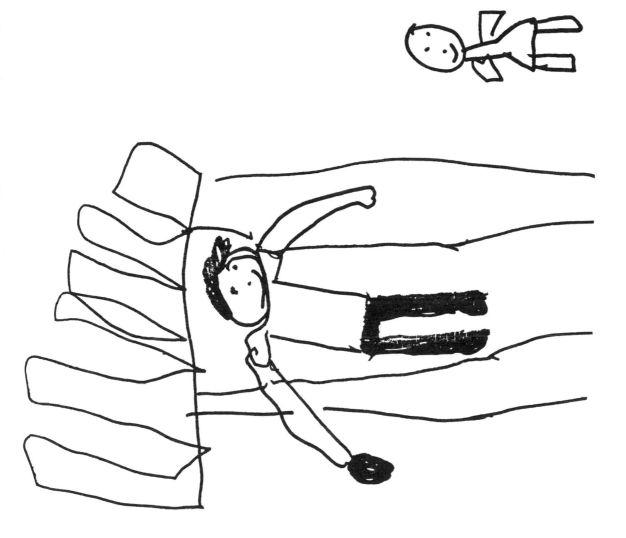

My dad and I go bowling.

Draw a picture of something you like to do with your mom.

I'm planting a garden with my mother.

i like to go fishing with my mom.

63

CHAPTER 3

Divorce

Most separations lead to divorce. A divorce is when two people decide they will no longer be married. They can't live together happily anymore. They agree to stop being husband and wife, but they are still parents to their children.

Draw a picture of divorce.

when my parenTS goT divorced, the whole house felT Sad.

70

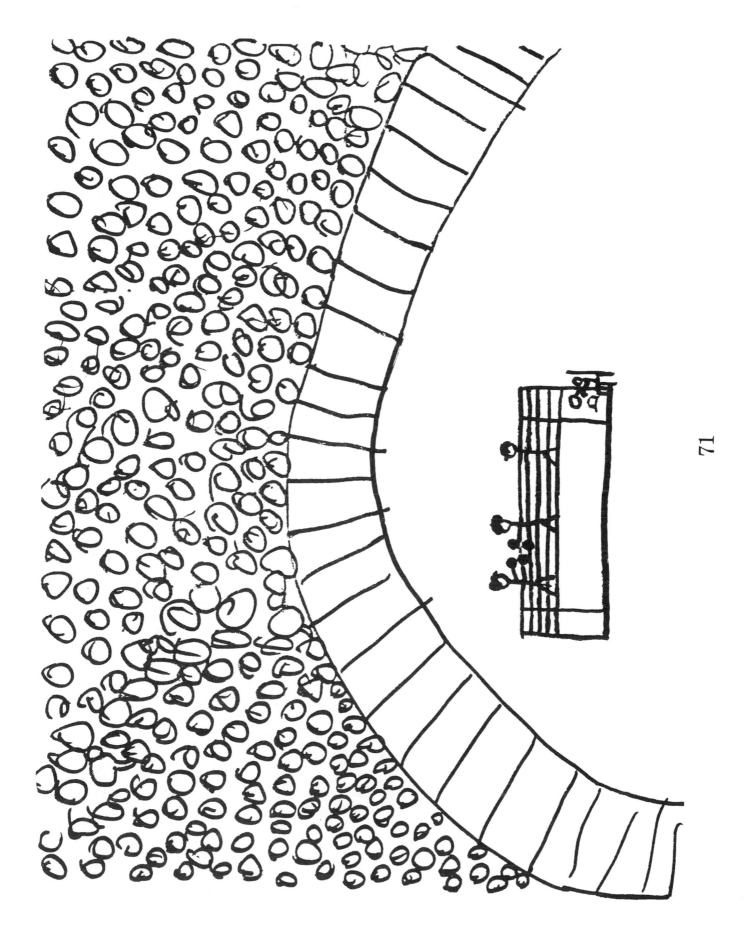

71

Divorce isn't easy. Parents may still argue a lot, like about where you should live.

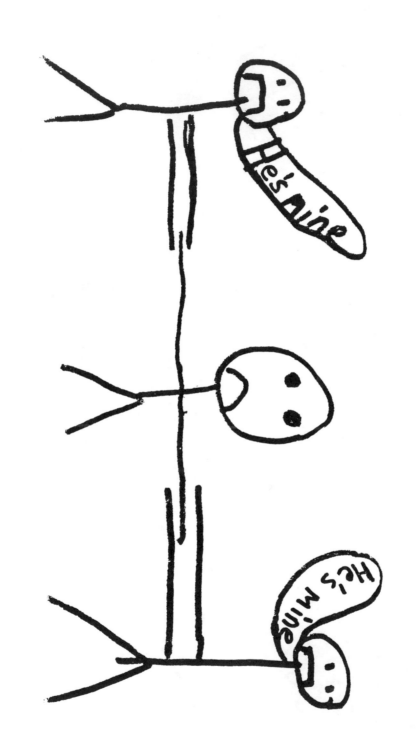

Don't think it's your fault

oh it's all my fault

73

All divorces have rules. There are rules about where the children will live, who gets what, visiting, and phone calls. It may be hard for parents to agree on the rules for the divorce. They may need help from family counselors, lawyers, or judges.

74

When a divorce happens, lots of things change. But lots of things stay the same.

What things stayed the same in your family?

75

I still don't like to clean up my room. That hasn't changed!

My mom's still my mom and my dad's still my dad.

Draw a picture of yourself.

I haven't really changed.
I'm still the same person.

79

CHAPTER 4

New Families

After a divorce, the changes may not be over. Your mom or dad may have a new boyfriend or girlfriend. One or both of your parents may get married again. If this happens you are in a new kind of family, called a stepfamily.

83

When your mother marries someone
Who is not your father or your
Father marries someone who is
not your mother, you are in a
Step family.

84

Has your mother or father remarried?
Draw the wedding here.

There are a few ways to become part of a stepfamily.

- A single parent may remarry after a divorce.

- A single parent may marry for the first time.

- A parent may get married again after a husband or wife has died.

88

Draw a stepparent.

Draw a stepfamily.

91

If one of your parents has a baby with a person who is not your other parent, that child is your half brother or half sister. If your stepparent already has a child, that child is your stepbrother or stepsister.

93

Sometimes another grown-up moves in with one of your parents, but they don't get married, at least not right away. Even though they are not married, this is another kind of family.

Michael is my mom's boyfriend. He lives with us. He's part of our family.

95

Kids have many questions about new families.

What do I call my mom's boyfriend?

How come my mother and stepmother don't get along?

Do I have to love my new stepdad?

Do I have to listen to my stepbrother when
he tells me what to do, just because he's older?

Where am I going for Thanksgiving?

I call my stepmom mom,
because she is my stepmom,
even though she is my stepmom
I still call her mom.

What questions do you have about new families?

New families mean a lot of changes. Some of these changes may be hard and confusing.

It's hard having two different rooms.
One doesn't really feel like home.

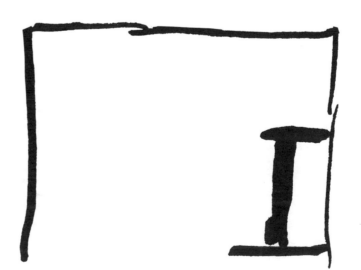

It's confusing when people in the same home have different last names.

Just when I get used to my dad's house
I have to go back to my mom's house.

First my mom and dad got divorced, then they both got remarried. Now I have a mom, a dad, a stepmom, a stepdad, and eight grandparents!

104

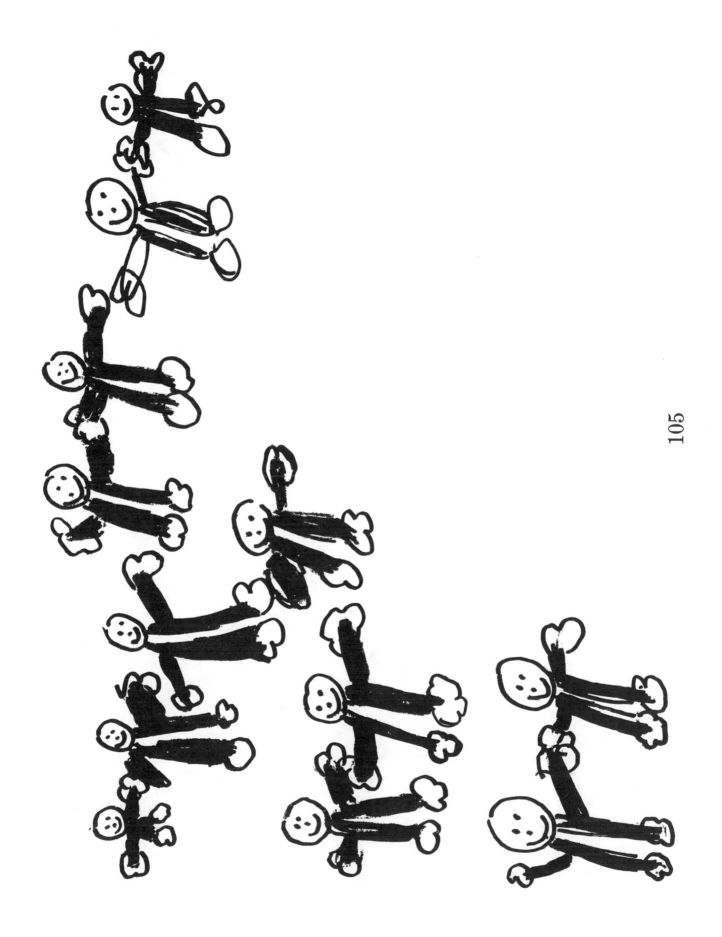

My father's new family
has four kids. I hope
he doesn't forget about
me.

Now I have a stepbrother. We're in the same class. We're both tired of explaining things to people.

I don't want a stepfather. He could change his mind and go away.

Sometimes it's hard to know who to listen to.

My Dad is happier since he got married again. He doesn't yell so much.

Different families may have different rules.

What are some of the rules in your mom's house?

110

What are some of the rules in your dad's house?

I'm The Boss because this is my house.

We both own the house so we're both boss.

Sometimes new families have new babies.

Are there any babies in your family?
Draw them here.

First my mom got remarried. And that was O.K. But then she had a new baby. that part I didn't Like!

The new baby.

115

CHAPTER 5

Feelings

Kids have many feelings about becoming part of a new family.

Circle some words that show how you feel. Add any others you wish.

- Confused
- Safe
- Worried
- Sad

- Angry
- Lonely
- Embarrassed
- Weird

- Happy
- Scared
- Ignored
- Jealous

- Relieved
- Lucky
- Guilty
- Different

- Loved
- Normal
- Hopeful
- Excited

- _____
- _____
- _____

119

Draw a picture of a feeling.

Scared

Sometimes I feel like a grump.

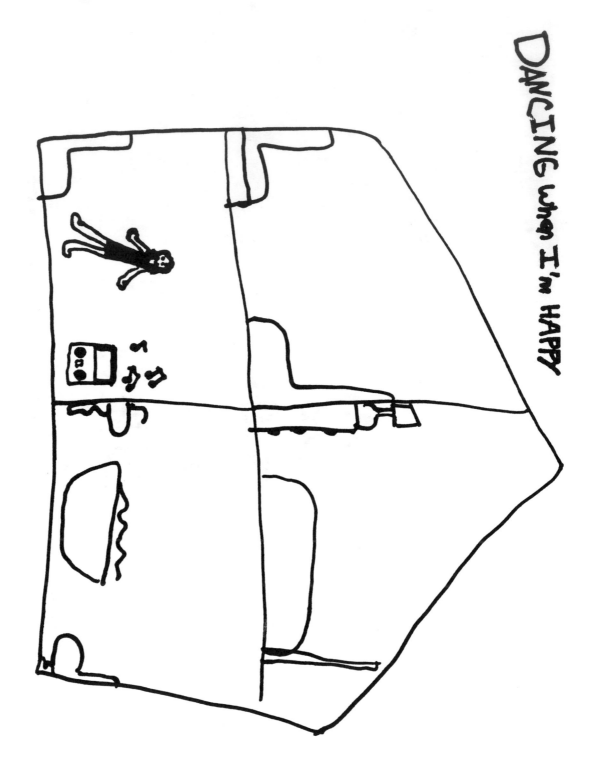

DANCING when I'm HAPPY

They tell you that after the
divorce, you'll be happier.
Then if you're sad, it's hard
to tell them.

125

I feel lonely.

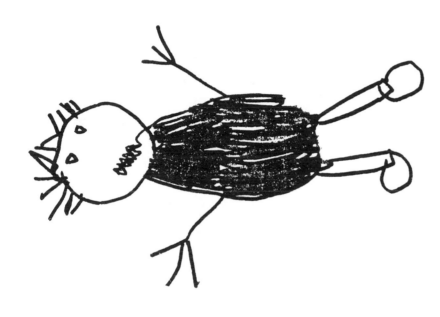

Sometimes I just get angry
about everything.

Sometimes I feel like pulling my sister away from her new boyfriend.

I don't like having to share my mom.

Some Times
I have a lot
on my mind.

When I am
When my mom
and
Dad sends
me to my room
I don't
Like
his
Rules

I can't
wait I get
used to it.
it
is OK

If you're feeling sad
it's ok to cry.

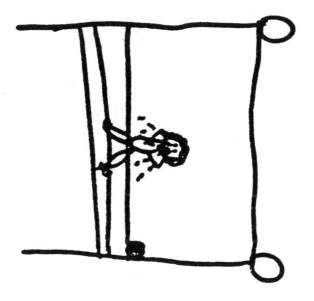

It was weird to go to my dad's wedding.

133

It's hard for me when my Dad picks
up His new wife's Little girl and swings Her
around. I grew up being the youngest and He
used to swing me around like that. Now I'm too
Big and I feel jealous. It's not easy having
Someone else be the youngest.

135

Now it's weird. Everyone gets along
Too well and I'm still mad!

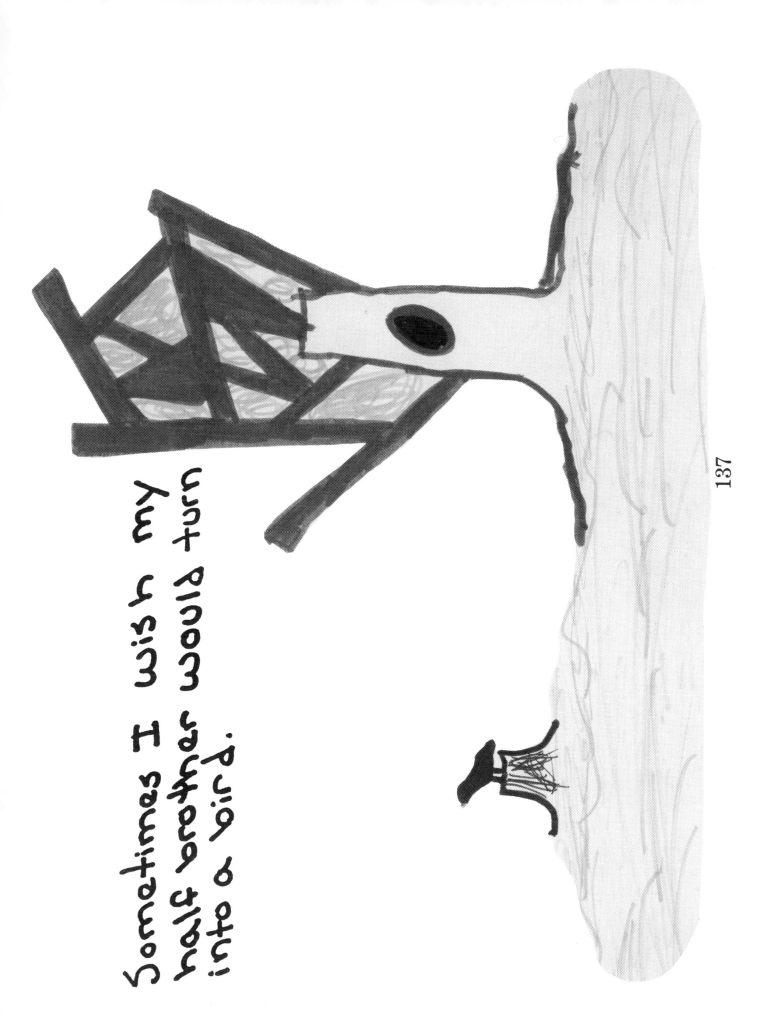

Sometimes I wish my half brother would turn into a pig.

What kinds of feelings do you have about the changes in your family?

Sometimes it's hard being in two families at once.

140

My one family

Dad

Me

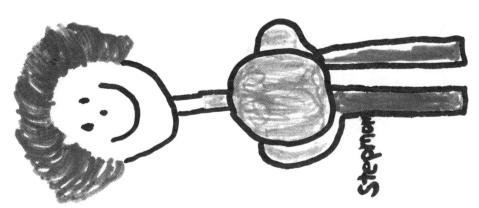

Stephanie

step dad

Mom

me

My other family

142

Even though some of the changes are hard, there are lots of good things about new families.

What I like about being in a step family is
That I got a new baby sister.

144

I like my mom's boyfriend. It's fun to do things together.

Stepfamilies are wonderful. More presents at Christmas. More people to love. New families, new friends, new sisters, new brothers, new pets, and always someone to talk to!

It's fun to ride bikes with my Dad and his girlfriend.

147

My stepdad is teaching me to play football.

What things do you like about your new family or families?

CHAPTER 6

Helping Yourself

Kids have lots of good ideas that can help when a family is changing.

Talk with your sisters and brothers privately.

Talk to your parents about your feelings.

Cheer each other up!

155

If you are upset or confused, you can also talk to your teacher, a counselor, a relative, or a friend.

My aunt and I are swinging on the swings and talking.

157

I like to go for a walk.

158

My parents got divorced, and then my mom got married again. I have a new step brother. My dad's still not married. I get to see him every weekend. Sometimes I still get sad about the changes in my family, but most of the time, it's just one part of my life. Usually, I think about my friends, my school work, and riding my bike.

I talk to my best friend when
I have a problem.

161

It makes me feel good to call my
Mom on the phone and let her
know what I am doing.

162

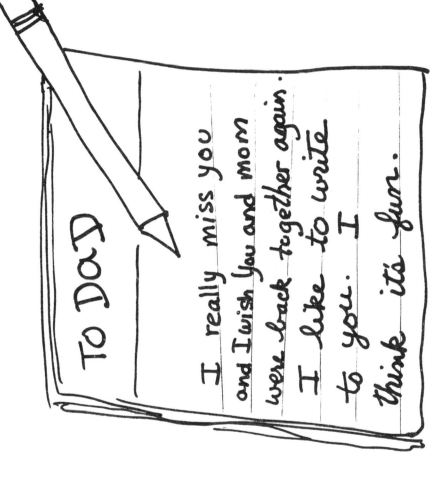

When I don't see my Dad,
I write him a letter.

163

When you feel sad, it
helps to have a hug.

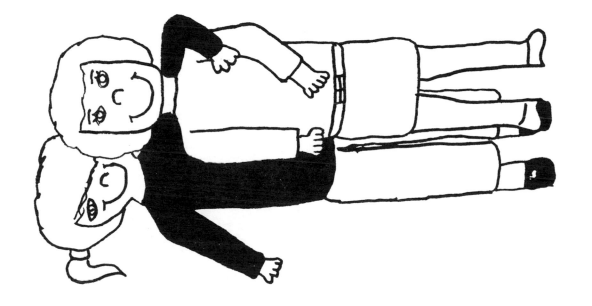

Get to know the new person in your family. Ask them lots of questions!

Have fun!

Don't let the divorce stop you from having fun.

Draw a picture of something you like to do with your family.

170

What advice do you have for grown-ups in new families?

Don't split up brothers and sisters. They need each other.

Don't be too pushy!

Explain any NEW RulesToThe Children.

Don't be too nice. Be yourself.

Don't bring gifts to she Ride to
make them like you.

New families don't always get along at first. It may take time to get to know each other.

174

Express your feelings

with your parents and/or step parents!

I think I'm going to get along with my step parents!

175

These pages are for you to make up stories or poems or draw any other pictures you want.

176

179

THE AUTHORS

David Fassler is a graduate of the Yale University School of Medicine. He completed his training in adult psychiatry at the University of Vermont, and in child psychiatry at Cambridge Hospital. He is an Instructor in Psychiatry at Harvard Medical School. Dr. Fassler is currently in private practice in Burlington, Vermont.

Michele Lash received her M.Ed. in expressive art therapies from Lesley College. She is currently affiliated with the Graduate Art Therapy Program at Vermont College. A registered art therapist and psychoeducational consultant, she is in private practice in Colchester, Vermont.

Sally Blakeslee Ives received her Ph.D. from the Department of Human Development and Family Studies at Cornell University. A licensed child psychologist, Dr. Ives is a Clinical Associate Professor of Psychiatry at the University of Vermont. She is currently in private practice in Burlington, Vermont.

Special Issues for Kids!

THE DIVORCE WORKBOOK
A Guide for Kids and Families
Sally B. Ives, Ph.D., David Fassler, M.D., and Michele Lash, A.T.R.

"The volume takes children by the hand from marriage through separation, divorce and 'legal stuff' which defines such terms as custody, child support, divorce mediation, and visitation. It also devotes considerable attention to the emotional aftermath of divorce."
—**Nadine Brozan**, *The Sunday New York Times*

$12.95 paper, $16.95 plastic comb spiral
160 pages, illustrated by children. Ages 4-12

JOSH
A Boy with Dyslexia
Caroline Janover
Illustrated by Edward Epstein

This is an adventure story with a section of resources and facts about learning disabilities.

"In Josh, Caroline Janover has taken me into the mind and heart of A Boy with Dyslexia. We share his fears, tragedies, and triumphs. Must reading for all families who struggle with dyslexia."
—**Mary MacCracken**, educational therapist and author of *Lovey, Turnabout Children, and Circle of Children*

$7.95 paper, $11.95 hardcover.
100 pages, 15 illustrations. Ages 8-12

LUKE HAS ASTHMA, TOO
Alison Rogers
Illustrated by Michael Middleton

The story shows that asthma can be managed in a calm fashion. For the more than two million families who have children with asthma, this is an important message."
—**Thomas F. Plaut, M.D.**, author of *Children with Asthma: A Manual for Parents*

$6.95 paper.
32 pages, illustrated. Ages 3-7

PLAYFUL PERCEPTION
Choosing How to Experience Your World
Herbert L. Leff, Ph.D.

Playful Perception invites readers to break old assumptions and view the world in new ways.

$9.95 paper, $15.95 hardcover. Classroom & workshop materials available on request.

WHAT'S A VIRUS ANYWAY?
The Kids' Book About AIDS
David Fassler, M.D. and Kelly McQueen

AIDS can be a difficult subject to discuss with young children. However, children hear a lot about the disease at a very early age. *What's a Virus, Anyway?* is a simple introduction to help adults talk with children. The book includes children's drawings and questions, and provides basic information in a manner appropriate for 4-10 year olds.

"...that people with AIDS are just like everyone else, makes this book particularly distinctive."
—*Booklist*

$8.95 paperback, $12.95 plastic comb spiral
Ages 4-10. 70 pages. Illustrated by children.

Also, now a new Spanish edition:
¿QUE ES UN VIRUS?
Un libro para niños sobre el SIDA

MY KIND OF FAMILY
A Book for Kids in Single-Parent Homes
Michele Lash, A.T.R.,
Sally Ives Loughridge, Ph.D.,
and David Fassler, M.D.

Designed to help children express, explore and understand some of the special issues and feelings associated with living in a single-parent home.

$14.95 paper, $18.95 plastic comb spiral
208 pages, illustrated by children. Ages 4-12

CHANGING FAMILIES
A Guide for Kids and Grown-ups
David Fassler, M.D., Michele Lash, A.T.R. and Sally B. Ives, Ph.D.

This book helps children cope with the emotional confusion of being in a changing family. Divorce, remarriage, new surroundings, and new relatives are a few of the changes presented for discussion here.

"Many children of divorce openly or secretly hope that their biological parents will reunite. The new marriage shatters that illusion." —**David Fassler**, *"Parent & Child," New York Times*

$14.95 paper, $18.95 plastic comb spiral
192 pages, illustrated by children. Ages 4-12

LET'S TALK TRASH
The Kids' Book About Recycling
Kelly McQueen and David Fassler, M.D.

Children hear about oil spills, rain forests, and recycling on television and in school. They worry about the earth and personally feel the effects of pollution when a favorite beach is closed in the summer. *Let's Talk Trash* presents the problem of solid waste disposal for further thought and discussion among young children, their teachers or their parents.

"As a former teacher, I highly recommend this creative introduction to an important contemporary topic."
—**Constance Fornier, Ph.D., Texas A&M University**

"Never has 'talking trash' been so much fun! This book takes a refreshing look at a tough problem. I hope kids will share this book with their parents so that we all understand why it's important to protect our beautiful environment."
—**Madeleine M. Kunin, Governor of Vermont**

$14.95 paperback, $18.95 plastic comb spiral
Ages 4-10. 168 pages. Illustrated by children.

WATERFRONT BOOKS
98 Brookes Avenue, Burlington, VT 05401
Order toll-free: 1-800-639-6063